NEW JERSEY

Julie Murray

Big Buddy BOOKS
Explore the United States

VISIT US AT
www.abdopublishing.com

Published by ABDO Publishing Company, PO Box 398166, Minneapolis, MN 55439.

Printed in the United States of America, North Mankato, Minnesota.
042012
092012

♻ PRINTED ON RECYCLED PAPER

Coordinating Series Editor: Rochelle Baltzer
Editor: Sarah Tieck
Contributing Editors: Megan M. Gunderson, BreAnn Rumsch, Marcia Zappa
Graphic Design: Adam Craven
Cover Photograph: *Shutterstock*: Andrew F. Kazmierski.
Interior Photographs/Illustrations: *Alamy*: Prisma Bildagentur AG (p. 17); *AP Photo*: Cal Sport Media via AP Images (p. 27), Capitol Records (p. 25), John Marshall, JME (p. 25), North Wind Picture Archives via AP Images (pp. 13, 23), NYPL Picture Collection (p. 23), Scott Stewart (p. 25); *Getty Images*: Steve Dunwell (p. 19); *Glow Images*: Prisma RM (p. 19), Stock Connection (p. 27); *iStockphoto*: ©iStockphoto.com/aimintang (p. 26), ©iStockphoto.com/dolah (p. 26), ©iStockphoto.com/Kubrak78 (p. 11), ©iStockphoto.com/photog2112 (p. 27), ©iStockphoto.com/SDbt (p. 11), ©iStockphoto.com/DenisTangneyJr (p. 9), ©iStockphoto.com/Whiteway (p. 30); *Shutterstock*: Amanda Boutcher (p. 5), Steve Byland (p. 30), Songquan Deng (p. 21), Melinda Fawver (p. 30), K.L. Kohn (p. 9), Philip Lange (p. 30), SeanPavonePhoto (p. 29).

All population figures taken from the 2010 US census.

Library of Congress Cataloging-in-Publication Data

Murray, Julie, 1969-
  New Jersey / Julie Murray.
     p. cm. -- (Explore the United States)
  ISBN 978-1-61783-368-7
  1. New Jersey--Juvenile literature. I. Title.
  F134.3.M87 2013
  974.9--dc23
                                2012010554

New Jersey

Contents

ONE NATION

The United States is a **diverse** country. It has farmland, cities, coasts, and mountains. Its people come from many different backgrounds. And, its history covers more than 200 years.

Today the country includes 50 states. New Jersey is one of these states. Let's learn more about this state and its story!

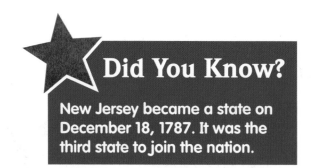

Did You Know?

New Jersey became a state on December 18, 1787. It was the third state to join the nation.

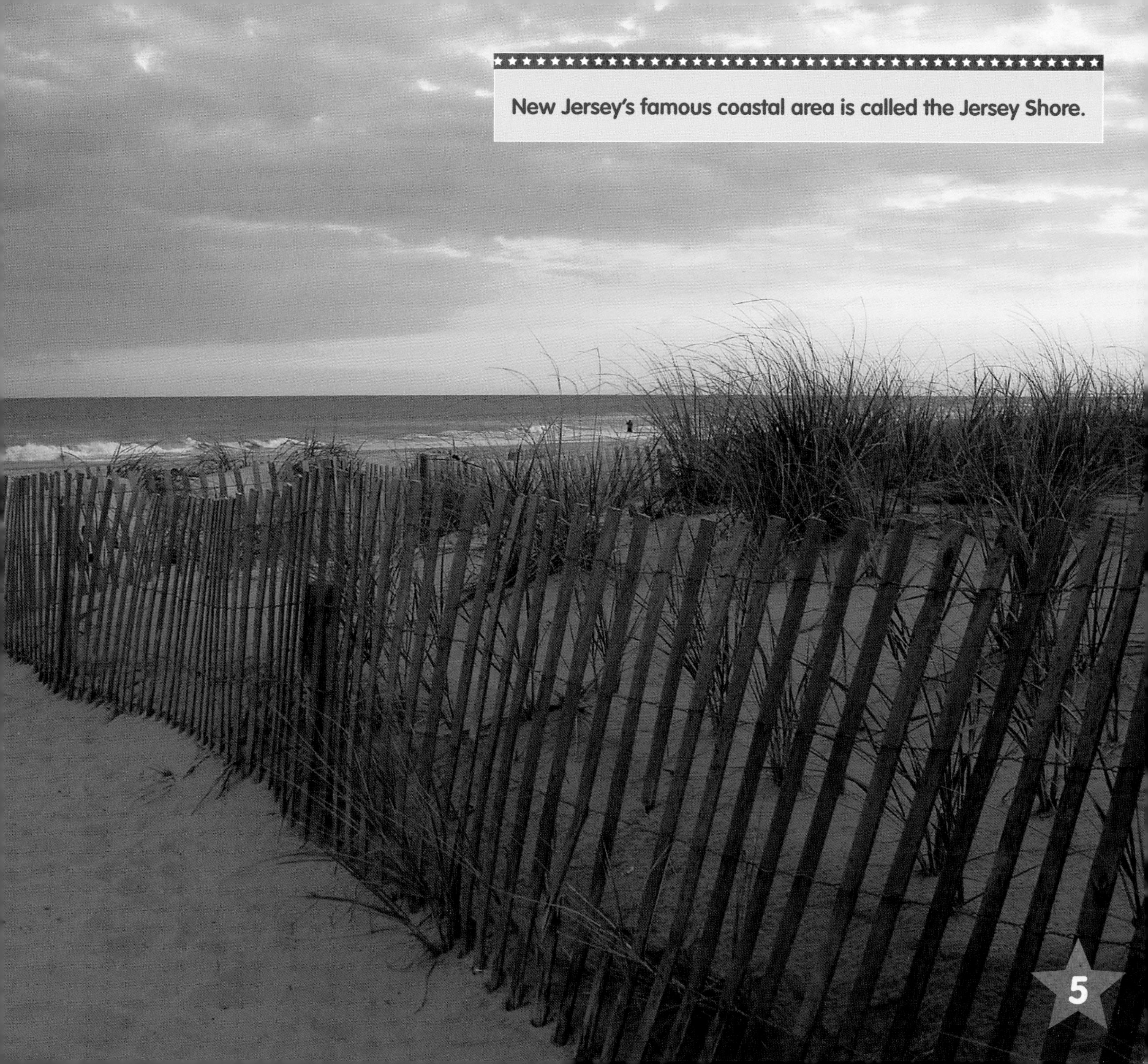

New Jersey's famous coastal area is called the Jersey Shore.

New Jersey Up Close

The United States has four main **regions**. New Jersey is in the Northeast.

New Jersey has three states on its borders. Delaware and Pennsylvania are west. New York is north. The Atlantic Ocean is east.

New Jersey is a small state with many people. Its total area is 7,812 square miles (20,233 sq km). Yet, about 8.8 million people live there.

REGIONS OF THE UNITED STATES

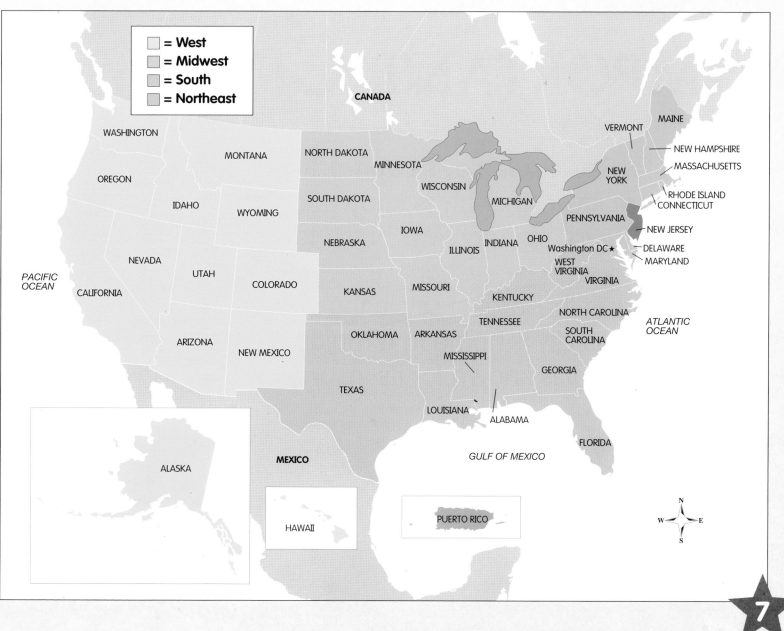

Legend:
- = West
- = Midwest
- = South
- = Northeast

CANADA

WASHINGTON

MONTANA

NORTH DAKOTA

MINNESOTA

OREGON

IDAHO

WYOMING

SOUTH DAKOTA

WISCONSIN

MICHIGAN

VERMONT

MAINE

NEW HAMPSHIRE

MASSACHUSETTS

NEW YORK

RHODE ISLAND

CONNECTICUT

PENNSYLVANIA

IOWA

NEVADA

UTAH

COLORADO

NEBRASKA

ILLINOIS

INDIANA

OHIO

Washington DC ★

NEW JERSEY

DELAWARE

MARYLAND

WEST VIRGINIA

VIRGINIA

PACIFIC OCEAN

CALIFORNIA

KANSAS

MISSOURI

KENTUCKY

NORTH CAROLINA

TENNESSEE

SOUTH CAROLINA

ATLANTIC OCEAN

ARIZONA

NEW MEXICO

OKLAHOMA

ARKANSAS

MISSISSIPPI

GEORGIA

TEXAS

LOUISIANA

ALABAMA

FLORIDA

ALASKA

MEXICO

HAWAII

PUERTO RICO

GULF OF MEXICO

N
W E
S

IMPORTANT CITIES

   Trenton is New Jersey's **capital**. It is located on the Delaware River. This city is known for its history. A famous **Revolutionary War** battle took place there in 1776.

   Newark is the largest city in the state. It has 277,140 people. This city is home to a major airport and many businesses. It is known for its **insurance** companies.

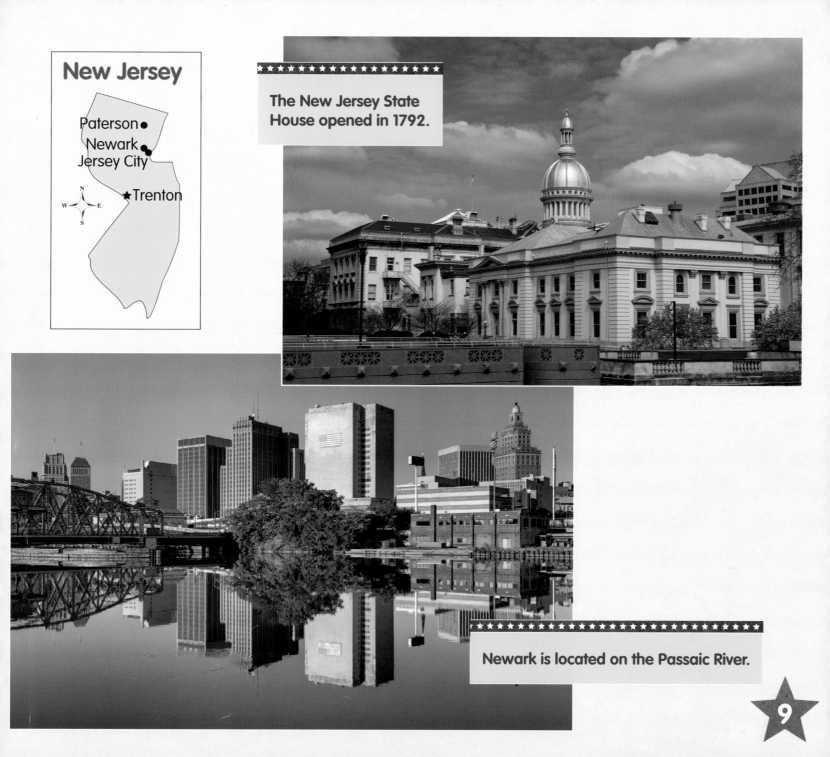

New Jersey

Paterson ●
Newark ●
Jersey City
★ Trenton

N W E S

The New Jersey State House opened in 1792.

Newark is located on the Passaic River.

Jersey City is the second-largest city in New Jersey. It is home to 247,597 people. It is close to New York City, New York. Companies in Jersey City make products such as clothes and electronics.

Paterson is the state's third-largest city, with 146,199 people. In the 1800s, it became known as "the Silk City" because silk was made there.

Did You Know?

Lambert Castle is a museum in Paterson. In 1892, it was built as the home of a silk factory owner.

Jersey City is on the Hudson River.

Great Falls near Paterson is known for its size. The falls drop down 70 feet (21 m)!

11

New Jersey in History

New Jersey's history includes Native Americans, explorers, and war. Native Americans have lived in present-day New Jersey for thousands of years. Europeans first explored the coast in 1524. Settlers arrived in the 1600s. Over time, the area became an English colony.

In the 1700s, colonists wanted to be part of a new country. So, they fought in the **Revolutionary War** and formed the United States. In 1787, New Jersey became the third state.

During the Revolutionary War, American soldiers crossed the Delaware River to reach Trenton. Their success at the Battle of Trenton gave Americans hope.

Timeline

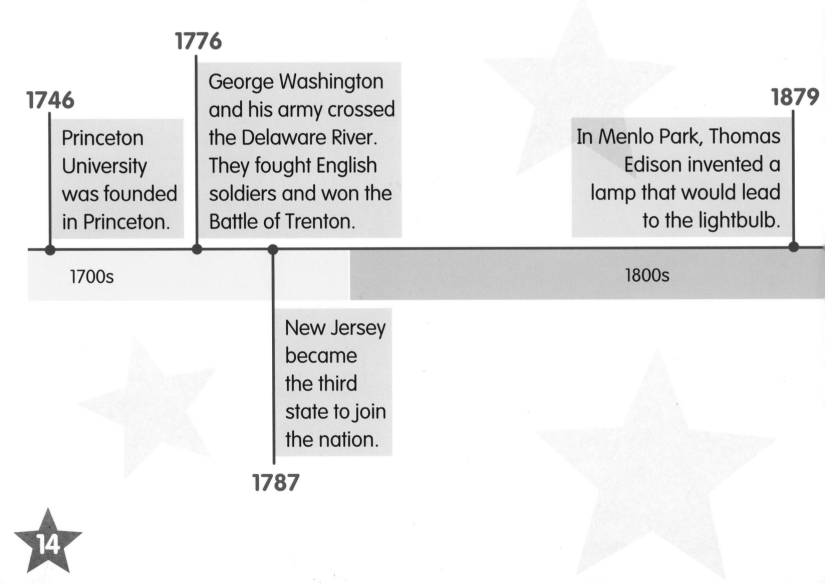

1746

Princeton University was founded in Princeton.

1776

George Washington and his army crossed the Delaware River. They fought English soldiers and won the Battle of Trenton.

1879

In Menlo Park, Thomas Edison invented a lamp that would lead to the lightbulb.

1700s

1800s

New Jersey became the third state to join the nation.

1787

1882

The first amusement park on a pier was built in Atlantic City.

1933

The country's first drive-in movie theater opened in Camden.

1994

Christine Todd Whitman became New Jersey's first female governor.

2011

Paterson Great Falls became the 397th US national park.

1900s

2000s

The first Miss America Pageant was held in Atlantic City.

The New Jersey Turnpike opened. It would become a major freeway.

On September 11, two airplanes hit the World Trade Center in New York City. About 650 people from New Jersey were killed in this attack.

1921

1951

2001

Across the Land

Did You Know?

In July, New Jersey's average temperature is 75°F (24°C). In January, it is 31°F (-1°C).

New Jersey has beaches, farmland, and mountains. It is nearly surrounded by water. The Atlantic Ocean is east. The Hudson River is northeast. The Delaware River forms the state's western border. It empties into Delaware Bay.

Many types of animals make their homes in New Jersey. These include ducks, mink, and skunks. Many kinds of fish and shellfish live in the coastal waters.

High Point is New Jersey's highest mountain peak. It is 1,803 feet (550 m) tall. It is in the Kittatinny Mountains.

EARNING A LIVING

New Jersey has many important businesses. Its companies make products such as electronics, food, and medicines. Some people have jobs helping visitors to the Jersey Shore. Many others work in nearby New York City.

Did You Know?

New Jersey mines produce different types of stone. Sand and gravel for building also come from the state.

New Jersey's farms raise dairy cows (*left*) and horses. Fruits, such as blueberries, are major crops from the state.

Boats from all over the world move goods through New Jersey's ports. This is important to US businesses.

19

NATURAL WONDER

Delaware Water Gap is a deep valley that cuts through the Kittatinny Mountains. The force of the Delaware River formed the valley over millions of years.

The Delaware Water Gap National Recreation Area is along the Delaware River. The park includes about 67,000 acres (27,000 ha) of land in New Jersey and Pennsylvania. People spend time there biking, camping, hiking, and river rafting.

Did You Know?

The Delaware River provides drinking water to millions of people.

The Delaware Water Gap is about three miles (5 km) long.

HOMETOWN HEROES

Many famous people are from New Jersey. Grover Cleveland was born in Caldwell in 1837. He was the US president two different times!

Cleveland was the twenty-second president from 1885 to 1889. He was the twenty-fourth president from 1893 to 1897. Cleveland is the only president who served a second term that was not right after the first term.

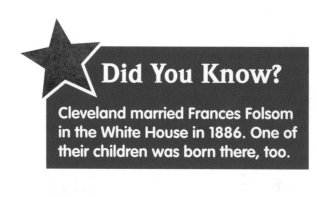

Did You Know?

Cleveland married Frances Folsom in the White House in 1886. One of their children was born there, too.

Cleveland worked to make sure the US government did not waste money.

People can still visit Cleveland's birthplace in Caldwell.

23

Many famous musicians are from New Jersey. Singer and actor Frank Sinatra was born in Hoboken in 1915. He became well known in the 1940s. He stayed popular for many years.

Two rock stars of the 1970s and 1980s are also from New Jersey. Bruce Springsteen was born in Freehold in 1949. Jon Bon Jovi was born in Perth Amboy in 1962. They both wrote and sang songs about New Jersey. One Bon Jovi album is even named *New Jersey*.

Did You Know?

Whitney Houston was another popular singer from New Jersey. She was born in Newark in 1963. Houston was also an actress.

Sinatra became popular for his love songs.

Springsteen is called "the Boss." One of his famous songs is "Born in the USA."

Bon Jovi is known for giving money to help people in need.

Tour Book

Do you want to go to New Jersey? If you visit the state, here are some places to go and things to do!

⭐ Play

Visit the Jersey Shore on the Atlantic Ocean coast. Explore its famous boardwalks. These are wooden paths near beaches. Some have rides and food!

⭐ Remember

Visit Washington Crossing State Park near Trenton. This is where the Battle of Trenton took place on December 26, 1776. Every year, locals act out the historic crossing of the Delaware River.

★ Ride

Cruise the New Jersey Turnpike. This famous road is 148 miles (238 km) long. It is 14 lanes wide in some places!

★ Cheer

See the New Jersey Devils play hockey in Newark.

★ Eat

Try some saltwater taffy. It was first made in Atlantic City in the late 1800s.

A GREAT STATE

The story of New Jersey is important to the United States. The people and places that make up this state offer something special to the country. Together with all the states, New Jersey helps make the United States great.

The George Washington Bridge connects New Jersey with New York City.

Fast Facts

Date of Statehood:
December 18, 1787

Population (rank):
8,791,894
(11th most-populated state)

Total Area (rank):
7,812 square miles
(46th largest state)

Motto:
"Liberty and Prosperity"

Nickname:
Garden State

State Capital:
Trenton

Flag:

Flower: Blue Violet

Postal Abbreviation:
NJ

Tree: Red Oak

Bird: Eastern Goldfinch

Important Words

capital a city where government leaders meet.

diverse made up of things that are different from each other.

insurance a contract that promises to guard people against a loss of money if something happens to them or their property.

region a large part of a country that is different from other parts.

Revolutionary War a war fought between England and the North American colonies from 1775 to 1783.

Web Sites

To learn more about New Jersey, visit ABDO Publishing Company online. Web sites about New Jersey are featured on our Book Links page. These links are routinely monitored and updated to provide the most current information available.

www.abdopublishing.com

Index